DEDICATED WITH LOVE

TO
MY CHILDREN
JEFFREY, JANET AND JOSEPH
AND
MY GRANDCHILDREN
NATALIE AND PATRICK

I LOVE HOLDING YOUR HANDS!

WITH NEVER ENDING LOVE
MOM
OR
GRAMMY
OR
JANIE JASIN

heart in hands

A Small Book About Giving and Receiving

Words by Janie Jasin

Photographs by Orin Ruchick

ISAIAH:

For you shall go out
in joy, and be led forth in peace:
the   mountains
and the   hills before
you shall   burst forth
into singing,   and all of
the trees of the field shall clap
their hands.

No one has your hands

NO ONE HAS THE SAME GIFTS AND HEALING MAGIC
IN THEIR HANDS AS YOU HAVE IN YOURS.
THERE ARE NO HANDS LIKE YOURS.

LOOK AT YOUR HANDS.

LOOK AT THE PALMS OF YOUR HANDS.

SEE THE MARKS, THE SCARS

AND THE LINES OF YOUR HANDS.

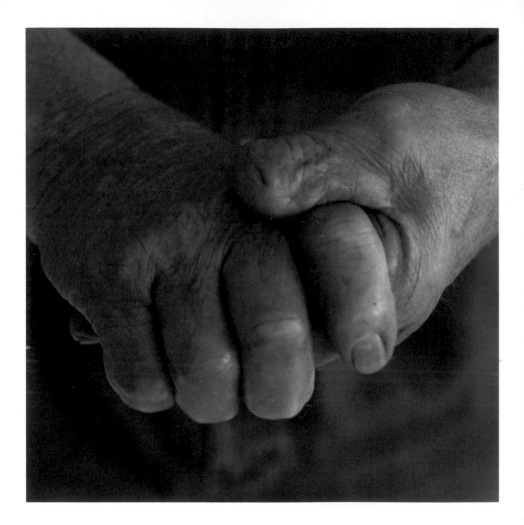

TURN YOUR HANDS OVER AND
SEE THE RINGS, SEE THE CHARACTER,
THE STRENGTH, THE BONES
AND FLESH OF YOUR HANDS.

THESE ARE YOUR HANDS.

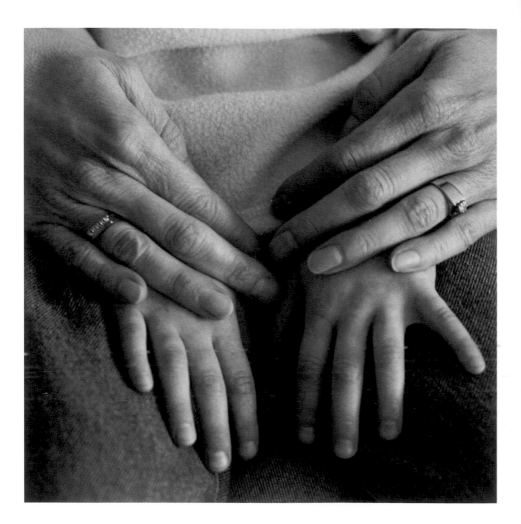

No one has your hands

HANDS THAT HOLD CHILDREN.

HANDS THAT HOLD YOUR SWEETHEART.

HANDS THAT HOLD GRANDCHILDREN.

No one has your hands

HANDS THAT COMFORT THE SICK AND DYING.

HANDS THAT WIPE TEARS AND NOSES.

HANDS THAT MAKE YOU FEEL SAFE.

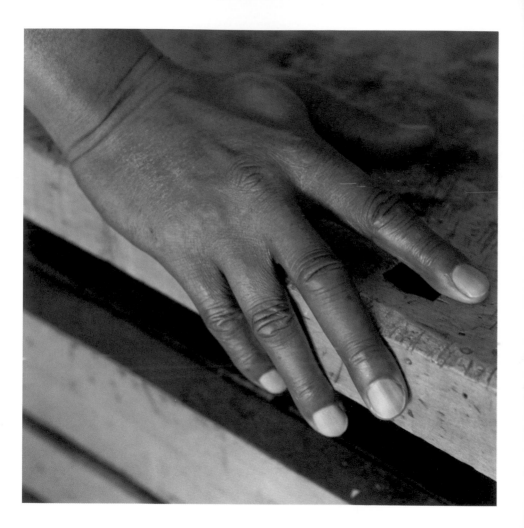

No one has your hands

HANDS THAT PLANT GARDENS.

Hands that prepare meals.

HANDS THAT FIX THINGS THAT ARE BROKEN.

HANDS THAT FOLD LAUNDRY .

No one has your hands

HANDS THAT TURN THE PAGES.

HANDS THAT PLAY THE PIANO.

HANDS THAT SKETCH AND DRAW.

No one has your hands

HANDS THAT NURTURE.

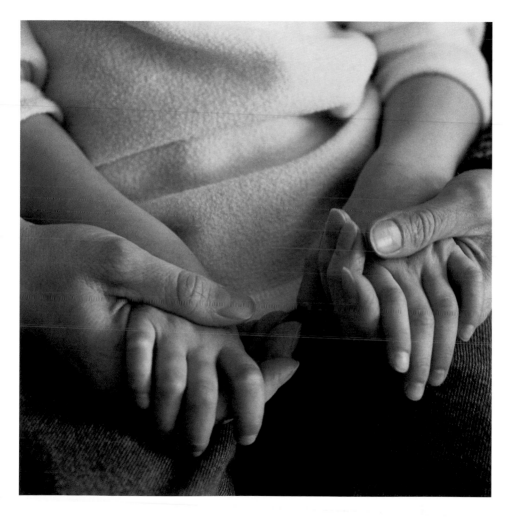

HANDS THAT SHAKE PAWS.

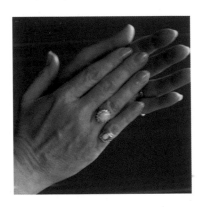

HANDS THAT APPLAUD.

No one has your hands

HANDS THAT HOLD KEYS.

HANDS THAT STEER THE AUTOMOBILE.

HANDS THAT PUSH A WHEELCHAIR.

HANDS THAT MAKE BREAD,
CAKES AND COOKIES.

No one has your hands

HANDS THAT HEAL.

Hands that massage.

HANDS THAT REHABILITATE.

No one has your hands

HANDS THAT GIVE GIFTS.

Hands that bring good to you.

HANDS THAT BRING GOOD TO OTHERS.

No one has your hands

HANDS THAT HOLD HANDS...

TO WALK...

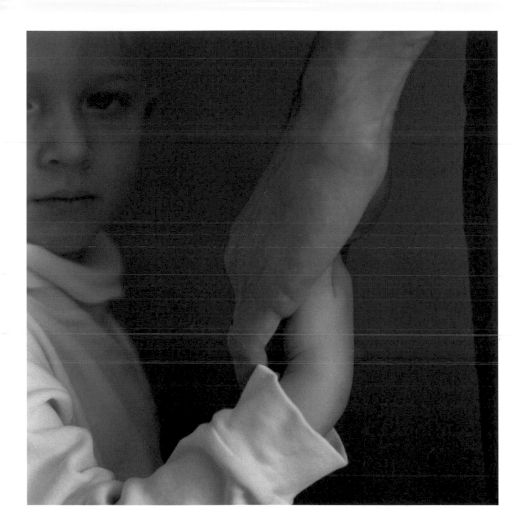

To pray...

TO FOLD IN GRATITUDE
AND THANKSGIVING.

No one has your hands

TAKE YOUR HANDS AND
PLACE THEM AROUND YOUR ELBOWS.
HUG YOURSELF GENTLY.

AND THEN...

WHEN YOU ARE READY...

TAKE YOUR HANDS AND PUT THEM

GENTLY AROUND SOMEONE ELSE.

"MANY HANDS ARE LAID UPON ONE LIFE"

Sidney Poitier

The heart in

Thank you for all of the hands that guided me safely
from childhood through adulthood.

Thank you to my godmother who chose
beautiful gloves for Sunday church.
Your hand in mine meant safety and love.

Thank you to my dear friends whose hands have helped me.

your hands has

Thank you for trained dogs that
fetch for those who cannot use their hands.

Thank you to those who hold hands praying in a circle.

Thank you for working men and women whose hands shape,
gather, weld, nurse, style hair and wait tables.

made a

Thank you to those audiences whose
applause affirmed my speaking vocation.

Thank you for the hands of care givers
that tended my aging parents.

difference in

Thank you to all who join hands helping others.

Thank you for hands that anoint and bless and serve
Rabbis, Priests, Ministers, Nuns and Chaplains.

Thank you for children's hands so
small that willingly hold mine.

my life.

JANIE JASIN

The Author

Janie Jasin

JANIE JASIN is a motivational speaker
and the author of the bestselling
Christmas classic, *The Littlest Christmas Tree*
and *If Love is Contagious I Hope You Never Get Well.*
She lives in Victoria, Minnesota

The Photographer

Orin Rutchick

ORIN RUTCHICK is an art director,
graphic designer and professional photographer
who has worked on several other books including
Can We Try Again, finding a way back to love by Cheryl Karpen.
He Lives in Minneapolis, Minnesota

No Limits Publishing is a subsidiary of Creativity "No Limits", Inc.
Ms Jasin can be contacted at the following for information
regarding other products and for potential speaking engagements

CREATIVITY "NO LIMITS", INC.
1743 Green Crest Drive
Victoria, Minnesota 55386
phone 952.443.3086
fax 952.443.3081
e-mail janiej@mm.com
www.janiespeaks.com
www.tremendoustimes.com

Mr. Rutchick can be reached at:

ORIN RUTCHICK PHOTOGRAPHY & DESIGN
718 Washington Avenue North Studio#607
Minneapolis, Minnesota 55401
www.orutchickphoto.com
www.editorialphotoimages.com
www.minneapolisphoto.com